Merry Christmas

A GULF COAST CHRISTMAS

by
Perry Guy

Printed in the United States of America

ISBN 978-1-68222-592-9 (Print)
ISBN 978-1-68222-593-6 (Ebook)

Acknowledgements

I would like to thank Bridget Starr Taylor for her incredible job illustrating this book as well as her work previously in my book ***TREASURES IN THE SAND*** which is the first of the series. All illustrations have copyrights and are the intellectual property of Bridget and may not be used without her permission. You can find Bridget and more of her work at Melissa Turk Studios (www.melissaturk.com).

I would also like to thank my dearest friend, wife and editor, Tami Curtis, for her assistance with the book. Tami is an artist and owner of Tami Curtis Studios located at 3100 Roberson Rd., Bay St. Louis, MS 39520 (tamicurtisstudios.com). Tami is a celebrated artist in the Louisiana area as well as much of the South and her work is simply amazing. Please visit her store or her web site to view her work and thank you for supporting an independent Gulf Coast Artist!

It was late November on the Gulf Coast
And Beach Bunny in the marsh by the sea
Was preparing the Christmas social for his friends
All felt joy and excitement to decorate the tree

There is a seasoned Grand Ole Cypress
That adorns the bayou of a nearby stream
This sacred tree near Beach Bunny's home
Is where they celebrate the Immaculate birth
Of Jesus Christ, the Precious Holy Child King

A gentle Fall Sun smiled kindly
Upon the chilled early morning ground
Preparing a comfortable setting
For the festive gathering that was bound

First arrived Bama Beach Mouse
Along with his beach buddy Gusty Ghost Crab
They brought a magnificent fossilized starfish
Gusty had on loan from the Dauphin Island Sea Lab

Soon to follow a trio of pelicans gently gliding
Landing smoothly on the misty marsh runway
Adorned atop their heads colorful Christmas hats
The trio well known for their humor and love of play

Their burgeoning pouches full
With fresh catch from a bayside cove
Salty oysters, blue crab and brown gulf shrimp
Made up a tasty traditional seafood gumbo

A group of petit Sandpipers rapidly raced
Along the waterline of the sleepy stream
Their tiny legs moving faster than needles
Stitching a quilt on Maw Maw's Singer sewing machine

The Sandpipers were adorned with necklaces
That streamed from the neck down to the feet
Made from shells of unfortunate Sand Augers
That failed to make a timely retreat

Cuddly Caleb the Bayou Beaver
Was the next Christmas party guest to arrive
With his spouse, the lovely Betty Beaver,
And young ones close by her side

As a family of natural herbivores
They brought wild turnips and tasty greens
Gopher fruit, native acorns, maple bark
And sweet muscadine jelly made up a delightful vegan cuisine

There was a bit of wonderment about the guests
When Felix the Fox bashfully arrived
But he vowed to a pescatarian diet
And assured his commitment would not be compromised

This is a wondrous time of year
When a Spirit of Peace is more present than all
We shall joyfully celebrate this time
And let not our differences hinder this peaceful resolve

So, everyone gathered around
the Grand Cypress
And began to dress the barren tree
With unique and delightful
Christmas décor
Heirlooms past down from each
guest’s ancestry

The Pelicans brought a long string of shiny pearls
And wrapped around full measure of the tree
The pearls bore a brilliant glow
Caused from seasons of polishing by sand and sea

The Sandpipers attached oblong sand dollars
To the colorful necklaces they wore
They dyed them playful colors
Purple, pink, gold and sea blue azure

Caleb the Bayou Beaver carved magnificent woodwork
Depicting Baby Jesus in the manger low
Using enchanting driftwood
Creating a scene of the Love that God did bestow

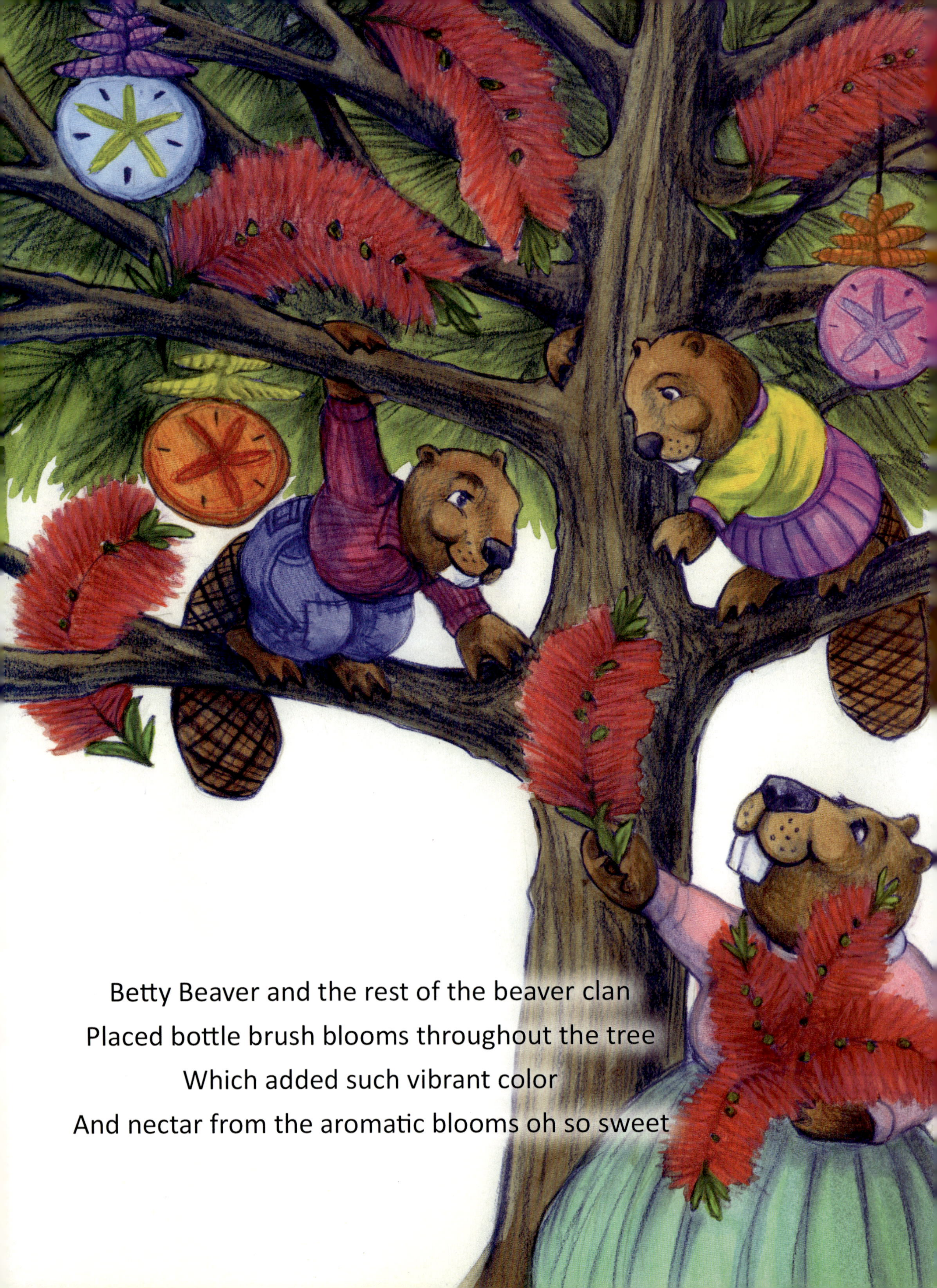

Betty Beaver and the rest of the beaver clan
Placed bottle brush blooms throughout the tree
Which added such vibrant color
And nectar from the aromatic blooms oh so sweet

Beach Bunny had prized Christmas shell ornaments
He would decorate the tree with every year
They were of various colors, shapes, and size
And did perpetuate joyful Christmas cheer

Beach Bunny knew in his heart
That Felix the Fox did not have ornaments of his own to bring
So, he shared his precious shells with Felix
And they decorated as a team

And now decorations were nearly done
Gusty and Bama climbed the trimmed tree
Placing the Majestic Starfish on top
It was the grandest ever to see

Then the most incredible
thing happened
As they admired the
work they had done
The last of the migrating
Monarchs gently landed
Enjoyed a taste of sweet nectar
and soon were gone

Their Christmas would be far across the Gulf
Somewhere on the Yucatan Peninsula in Mexico
The guests prayed them speedy and safe travels
And the Monarchs faded into the Fall Sun's soft glow

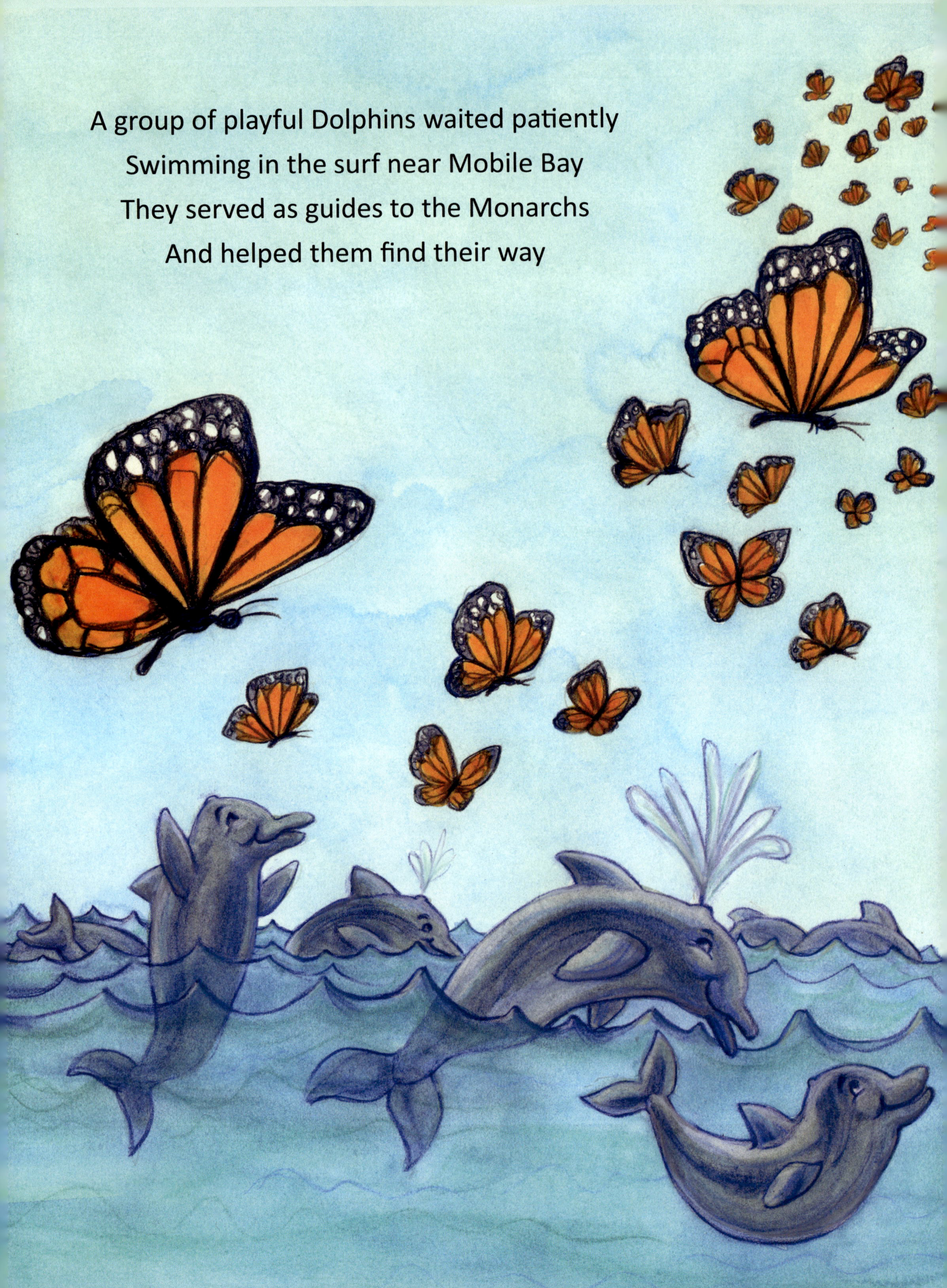
A group of playful Dolphins waited patiently
Swimming in the surf near Mobile Bay
They served as guides to the Monarchs
And helped them find their way

The Grand Ole Cypress adorned and decorated
Christmas festivities and dining complete
The content guests all headed toward home
To their own blessed humble retreat

No one was more grateful than Felix the Fox
His Heart so very full and life was good today
No one aware of his particular circumstance
Many times being shunned and turned away

Often, he is misunderstood because he is different
And spends much time by himself quietly at home
And this time of year could leave his heart sad
If while the community celebrates He is left alone

So, this Christmas if an acquaintance
Or perhaps a new friend you have yet to meet
Maybe an elderly person
Or a homeless soul living in the street
They may be dismayed and burdened with a hurt
Which has them quietly desperate,
alone, full of despair
Take a moment to share
the Love of the season
Let them know someone does truly care

And This Hope is still alive
This Hope is burning bright and strong
This Hope that once lay calm in a lowly manger
Now the Light of the World
Is calling to lead them safely Home

REMEMBER THE REASON FOR THE SEASON

MERRY CHRISTMAS FROM THE GULF COAST

THE PROPHECY

ISAIAH 7:14

Therefore, the Lord Himself will give you a sign: Behold, The Virgin shall conceive and bear a Son, and shall call His name IMMANUEL (God with us).

THE IMMACULATE CONCEPTION

MATTHEW 1: 20-21

But while he thought about these things, behold, an Angel of the Lord appeared to him in a dream saying, "Joseph, son of David, do not be afraid to take to you Mary your wife, for that which is conceived in her is of the Holy Spirit. And she will bring forth a Son, and you shall call His name Jesus, for He will save His people from their sins.

ETERNAL LIFE THROUGH FAITH IN JESUS CHRIST

JOHN 3:16

For God so Loved the world that He gave His only begotten Son, that whoever believes in Him should not perish but have everlasting life.

Lagniappe Section

noun

la • gniappe

\'lan'yap

a small gift given to a customer by a merchant at the time of a purchase; broadly: something given or obtained gratuitously or by way of good measure.

"A little something extra."

The Sandpiper

The Sandpiper stood firmly
With his back to the wind
No option but to endure
And pray the storm to end

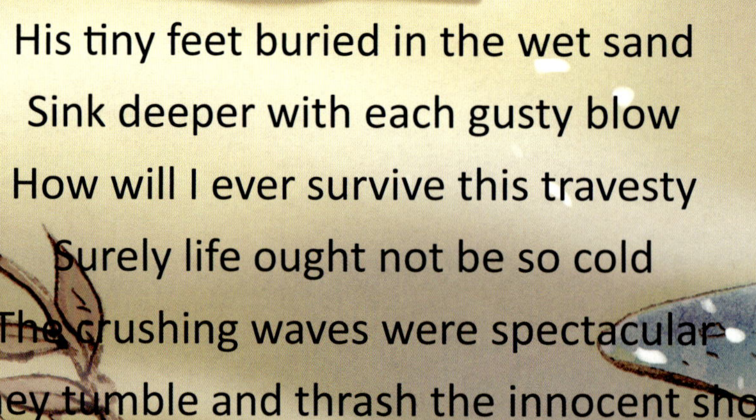

His tiny feet buried in the wet sand
Sink deeper with each gusty blow
How will I ever survive this travesty
Surely life ought not be so cold
The crushing waves were spectacular
As they tumble and thrash the innocent shore

The wind and rain made a haunting cry
The small Sandpiper had not heard before
For he was a juvenile bird
And not yet a cold season had he seen
And this wintry blast was a very frightful thing

Birds of a feather, how they flock together
Now I think I understand
As the Sandpipers all huddled around
Protecting each other from the blasting sand

And although he was young and strong
And holding fast to the front line
He felt the weakening of his tiny legs
Afraid he may fall in time
The other birds saw him fragile
And about to give in
They stood to each side and front
To hinder the blusterous wind

Soon the frigid rain stopped
And the furious winds ceased
The birds too exhausted to sing
However so grateful and graciously relieved
It was a most difficult experience
But now I understand
I can weather the most fierce of storms
With friends close at hand
The next year the winter storms came
The Sandpiper stood firmly facing the wind
Enduring and holding fast with confidence
Knowing that the storm would soon end

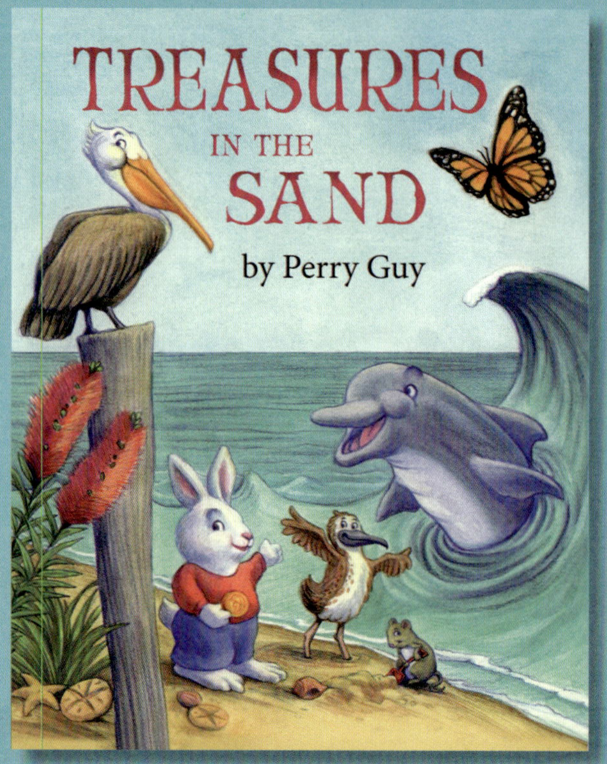

Treasures In The Sand

Treasures In The Sand is the first of the series and is a "must have" if you do not yet own it.

This book consists of ten short story beach poems written by Perry Guy and illustrated by artists from Melissa Turk Studios in New York. Building family values, learning to appreciate nature in life through charming characters, and being inspired through the written word are just some of the ideas we hope these books deliver. But above all, developing connections with God, family, and community are the most important goals, because ultimately the only things which have true lasting value are our relationships.

Visit **ThePainterAndPoet.com** to purchase your hard cover or download, as well as arrange a book signing with author Perry Guy.

The Mardi Gras Boat Parade

A new adventure starring all of your favorite animal characters from **Treasures In The Sand** and **A Gulf Coast Christmas**, also introducing a few new cuddly Gulf Coast creatures!

The Mardi Gras Boat Parade is written by Perry Guy and illustrated by artist Tami Curtis (TamiCurtisStudios.Com), a Gulf Coast native whose talents bring the book to life.

When exploring the Bay St. Louis area in Mississippi, please visit her studio where you will find her prints and original illustrations of The Mardi Gras Boat Parade. There you will also discover her other fine artwork showcasing the nature and culture of the Gulf Coast

To order books and arrange book signings for schools, libraries, and events; please visit: **ThePainterAndPoet.com**

Pearls Of Grace
by, Perry Guy
The pearls of dew
Align the spider's web of silk,
Exposing the trap
laboriously predawn the spider built.
The devious plot
Of malicious intent,
Avails no spoils
For effort spent.
So the architect retreats
To a more formidable space,
But heed tomorrow little fly,
Today you have pearls of Grace.